Discover birds with photos, fun facts, and verse

BIRDS
Discovering North American Species

Written by Dr. Shirley Raines

Photography by Curt Hart

Integrating science and art creates a valuable and unique learning experience that particularly benefits the youngest of readers. STEAM (science, technology, engineering, art, and mathematics) education inspires a wider audience to invest in studying subjects from multiple perspectives and promotes an education that suits many types of learners.

In this introduction to North American birds, artistic and scientific elements are combined to create a comprehensive learning experience for young readers.

Continue the learning with a selection of engaging exercises in the back of the book. These Story S-t-r-e-t-c-h-e-r-s© by Dr. Shirley Raines expand the material with a variety of activities perfect for learning both in and out of the classroom.

Robin in View

From my window I saw a robin
in the garden, near the feeder.

He perched on branches,
hopped on the grass, and
pecked at the fallen leaves.

I saw his yellow beak,
layers of pin feathers,
and bobbing black head.

The prettiest part of the robin
was his bright,
bright red chest.

Wait, wait, robin redbreast!
Where's your mate?

There she is. I spot her now,
rusty red on her chest.

Pretty mate,
please stay,
with your coat of rusty red.

I crept outside,
trying not to make a sound.
I searched for their nest.

Playing hide-and-seek
just to see their eggs
for a tiny peek.

I saw them, too.
Their eggs are robin's egg blue!

You Look Familiar

American robins are known for their red coloring, but they weren't the first to sport this look. When early settlers arrived in America, they noticed birds with bright red feathers, which reminded them of European robins, a bird with striking similarities to the robin we know and love. Since the American robin's coloring was so similar, the settlers gave the bird its name, even though American robins are actually a type of bird called a thrush.

Baby robins don't initially have their well-known red feathers.

Robins are the first songbird you are likely to hear in the spring.

American robins are one of a few bird species that can both walk and hop.

Blue Jay, Blue Jay

Blue jay, blue jay,
strut your stuff!

Blue jay, blue jay,
never gets enough.

Blue jay, blue jay,
what a sight!

Belly full of seeds and grain.
Scaring others, what a pain!

Beauty and Brains

Blue jays are known for their beautiful blue-violet coloring, but did you know they are also very smart? They know a wide variety of songs and sounds, and they are even known to mimic hawks! Blue jays have been said to use their hawk calls to scare away other birds from feeders, which means more food for them! They are also known to stick together at the first sign of trouble. If a blue jay in danger calls for help, nearby blue jays will recognize the call and fly in to save the day!

Blue jays use their crest to communicate their feelings. Crest up means upset or afraid, and crest down means relaxed.

Blue jays are said to be able to recognize each other by the black bridle across their throat.

Blue jay feathers aren't actually blue! Blue jays have special feathers that reflect light in a way that makes them appear blue.

Hey, Little Chickadee

Hey, little chickadee,
oh, so sweet.
Hey, little chickadee,
peep, peep, peep.

Hey, little chickadee,
hop, hop, hop.
Hey, little chickadee,
won't you stop?

Hey, little chickadee,
peep, peep, peep.
Hey, little chickadee,
you're so sweet!

Singing Sensations

The chickadee is a very vocal songbird. They are said to have many different identifiable songs and calls. You'll know you're listening to a chickadee when you hear their very distinct tune. It sounds just like their name!

Chickadees can fly up to 13 miles per hour (20.9 kilometers per hour).

Carolina chickadees are very agile and can even hang upside down on tree branches.

Chicakdees store food in many hiding places, but they are always able to remember where they left their meals.

Hummingbirds

· ·

We counted the hummingbirds
at the feeder today.
We wanted them to stay,
but as soon as they came,
they propelled away.

Going, Going, Gone

These tiny birds have wings that move so fast that they can hardly be seen. Males can flap their wings at speeds up to 200 times per second! In general, most hummingbirds flap their wings about 50 times per second. Not only are their wings moving at record-breaking speeds, they are flying faster, relative to their body size, than one of the fastest birds on the planet, the peregrine falcon. Not bad for a bird that weighs about as much as a nickel.

Hummingbirds can fly backward and even upside down!

Ruby-throated hummingbirds can consume up to 8 times their body weight.

Hummingbirds need to feed about every 10 minutes to maintain their constant movement.

Bird Headaches

Rat-a-tat-tat,
rat-a-tat-tat,
drumming a beat so loud.

Awake, O.K.
I'm awake,
hammer head!

Rat-a-tat-tat,
rat-a-tat-tat,
nailing your head to the bark.

Woodpecker, have you no song
to welcome the dawn
or just a hammering headache?

Knock, Knock

Woodpeckers are very inventive hunters. They use their powerful beaks to chisel out insects hiding under the bark of trees. They typically hammer against trees up to 12,000 times a day! Wondering how they don't get a headache? Their specialized beaks have a lot to do with preventing injury. They also have a sponge-like skull that securely surrounds their brain to keep it protected from all that hammering!

Downy woodpeckers have unusually long tongues and sticky saliva that they use to pull insects from trees!

Woodpeckers can be found on every continent except Australia and Antarctica.

Woodpeckers can peck up to 20 times per second!

A Mockingbird's Song

· ·

I awoke one morning and the birds
began to sing.
Their many songs in my head
started to ring.

As the birds sang their songs,
cheerful and long,
I whistled along to tell them I care.

Looked out my window.
Only one bird there.
Where have all the birds gone?

Oh, it was you mockingbird,
borrowing other birds' songs.

Re-Tweet

Mockingbirds sing long repetitions of songs, but not usually their own tunes. Sometimes they even mock other sounds they hear around their environment, like a rusty gate or meowing cat. Scientists have identified that mockingbirds can make up to 50 different call sounds. Some male mockingbirds can even learn up to 200 different songs! And unlike many songbirds who only sing during the day, mockingbirds sing almost all the time, even at night during the spring and summer.

Mockingbirds can imitate many sounds, including other birds, sirens, and even barking dogs!

The northern mockingbird is the state bird of 5 states in the U.S.

The white flashes on a mockingbird's wings make them look much larger than they actually are.

Red-Winged Blackbird on a Metal Post

. . . .

Red-winged blackbird
perched on a metal post.
Spanning your wings to catch the sun,
I think I like your colors the most.

Will you wait for another red-wing
or fly again to some other field?

Please stay here for me to see.
Just sit in the sun
with your beautiful wings.
I promise to watch your lazy fun.

Mismatched Mates

These beautiful
blackbirds with red patches
on their wings and a little strip of
yellow will often catch your eye. Not
only because of their beautiful coloring,
but because they are extremely common
across the United States. Their mates, however,
are not nearly as striking. Females are brown
with white stripes and tend to look more like
sparrows than their male counterparts.

Red-winged blackbirds have a poor sense of smell and rely heavily on their eyesight and hearing.

Male red-winged blackbirds don't develop their bright red patches and glossy black feathers until they are up to three years old.

Red-winged blackbirds are known as one of the most abundant birds in all of North America.

Bluebird Signs

· ·

They say the bluebirds have disappeared
from field and stream and farm.
Yet, yesterday, I saw them here
wiggling into a tiny box near the barn.
I watched them from far away,
wishing them no harm.
I do not want them to disappear
from field and stream and farm.

I saw fragile little eggs,
cracked and left behind.
I hope the hatchlings are nearby.
It would be a very good sign
for field and stream and farm
to see more bluebirds near the barn.

Comeback Kids

At one time, bluebirds
were almost extinct! After great
efforts from conservationists and bird
lovers alike, these beautiful blue beauties
have come back and evaded extinction! Friends
of the bluebird built special boxes for them to nest
in and helped keep track of their progress. These days,
bluebirds can be spotted in the open, particularly in
meadows and near farms across the eastern U.S.

Bluebirds have great eyesight and can see an insect over 50 yards (45.7 meters) away!

An eastern bluebird's diet mostly consists of insects and fruit. They rarely ever eat birdseed.

Bluebirds are considered a symbol of happiness. They have even been referenced in popular songs, such as "Somewhere Over the Rainbow."

Eleven Brown Pelicans Flying in a Row

Eleven brown pelicans flying in a row.
Ten brown pelicans swooping high and low.

Nine brown pelicans flapping their wings.
Eight brown pelicans diving for things.

Seven brown pelicans gobbling down their fish.
Six brown pelicans, what do you wish?

Five brown pelicans perching on a pier.
Four brown pelicans, can you see me here?

Three brown pelicans starting to fly.
Two brown pelicans swooping by.

One brown pelican flying high and low.
Zero brown pelicans, where did they go?

Look Out Below

Brown pelicans can almost always be found near coastlines searching for fish. They are expert fishermen and have a very unique approach. Unlike many of their pelican cousins, brown pelicans are known for flying just above the water until they spot a fish and then quickly "plunge-diving" into the water to scoop up their lunch in their pouch!

Brown pelicans have a pouch in their throats that they use to catch fish. Their pouch can hold approximately 3 gallons (11.3 liters) of water!

Brown pelicans are the smallest members of the pelican species.

Brown pelicans have air sacs under their skin and in their bones, which help them float in the water.

Who-o-o, Who-o-o

Who's that "who-o-oing" in the night?
That sound is giving me a fright!
Once again that "who-o-oing" sound,
but no one to be found.

Hopped in bed and off with the light.
"Who-o-oing" once again tonight?
Out of bed and on with the light.
Out to the porch, nothing in sight.

"Who-o-o, who-o-o,"
who's that "who-o-oing?"
Wink, winking, whose yellow eyes?
Blink, blinking in the night?

Owl, owl, you are quite a sight.
Perched up high, winking at my light.
I turned my flashlight on your eyes,
but you flew away into dark skies.

Who Goes There?

Owls are best known for their distinctive call, but they are also the reason people who like to stay up late are called "night owls." That's because owls are nocturnal, which means they typically sleep during the day and are more active at night. Owls have great vision and an excellent sense of smell making them great at finding food in the dark!

The tufts of feathers on a great horned owl's head are called "plumicorns."

Owls swallow their prey whole!

Owls are considered raptors, which means they have a hooked beak, great eyesight, and talons.

Caw-Cawing

· ·

Crows have a glossy black shine.
Feathers smoothly trimmed in line.

"Caw! Caw!" Across the glen.
When did this harsh song begin?

High up in the tallest tree today,
signaling birds far away.

"Caw, caw, caw," long and loud.
Coal black brow, oh so proud!

Something to Crow About

Crows are very vocal birds, and even though they aren't known for soft and sweet tunes like their fellow singing friends, they are still technically considered songbirds. Their most common vocalization is one you've likely heard a time or two. It is the familiar "caw, caw." However, crows use much softer songs when communicating with members of their family. They may not be the best singers, but each call has a unique meaning, making them excellent communicators!

American crows roost, or gather, in large groups in the winter. Thousands of crows can gather in one place!

Crows are really inventive and have been known for the clever ways they find food, such as making tools or tricking other animals out of their meals.

Crows have a bigger brain-to-body ratio of any other bird!

Where Do You Go
When it Snows, Canada Goose?

Where do you go when it snows,
Canada goose?
Where do you go?

Do you hide under the green bough
of the giant spruce?

Where do you go when it snows,
Canada goose?
Where do you go?

Do you fly away with your friends
making honking goose sounds?

Do you travel with your flock,
Canada goose?
Why do you fly in a V?

Where do you go when it snows,
Canada goose?
Where do you go?

Do you fly to warmer marshes?
Do you land on glassy ponds?

What do you eat
for your flight, big bird?
Where do you find corn or wheat?

Where do you go when it snows,
honking friend?
Where do you go?

Expert Travelers

Many Canada geese migrate south for the winter, but they don't go alone! They travel in groups called flocks. Some flocks fly up to 6,000 miles (9,656 kilometers) each year—they are expert travelers! The flocks fly in V-shaped formations, with one goose in the front and the rest flying slightly higher behind the leader. When the leader gets tired, they will honk and another goose will take their place!

Canada geese can fly between 40 and 60 miles per hour (64.3 and 96.5 kilometers per hour)!

A Canada goose's long neck helps them search underwater for food.

Baby Canada geese, or goslings, learn to swim the very first day they are born!

Cardinals on a Winter's Day

· ·

Five red cardinals sitting on a bush,
surrounded by morning's hush.

Four red cardinals in the cold,
pecking seeds from a dried bush bowl.

Three red cardinals casting a glow.
In the snow, would they stay or go?

Two red cardinals, a beautiful pair.
She was dull. He had red to spare.

One red cardinal greeted me today.
I left the seeds, then went away.

Now here alone I stay
hoping for cardinals on a winter's day.

The More the Merrier

These bright
red birds are sometimes
known for their cranky attitude
toward other cardinals—and even
other animals and people—but when
winter comes around, that all changes.
While in the summer months male cardinals
are protective of their mate and their area, in
the winter it becomes more important to stick
together. As the temperature drops, cardinals
flock! Some groups only grow by a few, but
others can be up to 70 strong!

Cardinals have a distinctive crest on their head that they only raise when they are upset, much like a blue jay.

Male cardinals are known for their bright red feathers, whereas females are typically light brown with just hints of red.

Both male and female cardinals are capable of singing, even though usually only male songbirds sing.

STORY S-T-R-E-T-C-H-E-R-S©

Stretch out the learning with this collection of activities created specifically to enhance the material and provide new ways to discover the wonderful world of birds. From language, to science, to art, to mathematics, each activity incorporates information from the book and provides a new approach to teaching early learners in and out of the classroom. For more Story S-t-r-e-t-c-h-e-r-s©, please visit www.FlowerpotPress.com.

Story S-t-r-e-t-c-h-e-r© for ART

What the children will learn
To match the color of robin's egg blue

Materials
Crayons the same color as robin's egg blue; photos of robin's eggs; strips of paper; scissors; paper clips; blue, yellow, and white paints; small paint brushes; watercolor paper or other white paper; and paper plates for palettes

What to do
1. Read the poem about robins and note the details about the color of the robin's egg.
2. Use the robin's egg blue crayon to color a small strip of paper.
3. Use a paper clip to attach the strip of paper to the painting paper.
4. Use the paper plates to mix colors and try to achieve the robin's egg blue color by combining mostly blue, a tiny bit of yellow, and white paint.
5. When they think it is a match, have them paint their paper to match the color strip.

Something to think about
Consider using home improvement or paint store paint samples for children to get the closest match to the robin's egg blue color.

Story S-t-r-e-t-c-h-e-r© for SCIENCE

What the children will learn
The habits of hummingbirds

Materials
Information about hummingbirds; pictures of hummingbirds; videos; straws; and juice boxes

What to do
1. Read the poem about hummingbirds and emphasize the "propelled away" part.
2. Show a short video of hummingbirds from the Internet. Help the children to see when the hummingbird propels away from a flower or feeder.
3. Discuss their size, how fast they are, and what they are eating from the flowers or the nectar feeders.
4. Have the children mimic the hummingbirds by flapping their arms as fast as possible while trying to insert a straw into their juice boxes to drink the juice or "nectar."

Something to think about
For older children, discuss the ways that people interested in hummingbirds attract them to a feeder. If possible, show children a hummingbird feeder.

Story S-t-r-e-t-c-h-e-r© for LISTENING/MATHEMATICS

What the children will learn
To listen for variation in birdcalls and songs

Materials
Information about mockingbirds; video or sound recording of a mockingbird; chart tablet or whiteboard; and markers

What to do
1. Read the poem about mockingbirds.
2. Teach children that mockingbirds imitate other birds' songs, sometimes singing as many as 12-16 different songs.
3. Secure a sound recording or a video of a mockingbird singing.
4. Have the children listen to a mockingbird's song and when the mockingbird changes his or her song, make a hash mark on the chart tablet or whiteboard.
5. Listen to the mockingbird again and have children make their own hash marks.
6. Count the number of songs they think they hear.

Something to think about
The important concept is the mockingbird imitates other birds and makes many beautiful bird songs.